Affirmations For Abundance

How to Create Wealth with Words

Jeanne Ellen Russell

Edinburg, Virginia

Copyright © 2011 Jeanne Ellen Russell
All rights reserved.

ISBN- 978-0-9830259-1-7
LCCN: 2011935901
Published by Winding Path Press

Dedication

This book is dedicated to my mom, who always had a positive attitude despite all the challenges of being a single mother trying to raise four happy children alone.

CONTENTS

	Acknowledgments	i
1	The Basics	1
2	Affirmations to Create Prosperity	5
3	Extra Tips on Creating Prosperity and Abundance	45

Acknowledgements

Thanks to Napoleon Hill, Jack Canfield, Barbara Winter, Tony Robbins and everyone else who taught me the value and power of affirmations.

1
The Basics

What are affirmations?

Humans are funny creatures. Our minds are always working, even when we are asleep. We send ourselves messages all day and all night, each and every day. Some messages are sent automatically and without thought, like when we tell ourselves to breathe and tell our hearts to beat. And some messages are sent consciously like when we decide what we're going to do on a certain day. And there are the messages that we send subconsciously. These messages are very powerful and if we choose, we can control them.

Affirmations are *positive* messages we send to ourselves. Many of us have been conditioned by experience to talk down to ourselves. We say things in our minds like, "Don't mess this up" or "Why can't you ever get things right?" Sometimes we're hearing the voice of a critic from our childhood or our own selves giving voice to our fears. Where these messages come from is not necessarily the important thing. The important thing is to notice and then replace the negative, fear-based thoughts with positive affirmations.

The affirmations in this book are designed to help transform your state from one of difficulty to one of abundance and prosperity.

How Should I use these affirmations?

This little book is meant to be pleasing and easy. Just read through the affirmations and notice how you feel. When you come across a particular affirmation that makes you feel good, repeat it. You can read them aloud or silently. You might even consider recording yourself saying your favorite affirmations while gentle music plays in the background. You can put this recording on when you sleep and let your dreams be filled with positive thoughts and messages.

If you meditate or exercise you can use these affirmations as a mantra to repeat over and over with your breath.

The more we learn about the human brain, the more we acknowledge the power of the subconscious mind. This is not magic, although sometimes the effects are just as powerful as magic.

Eventually you will want to create your own affirmations. Here are some tips to keep in mind.

- **State your affirmations in a positive manner.** The universe does not hear negatives. For example, let's say you want to stop wasting your money on junk food. If you say, "I am grateful that I've stopped spending money on junk food", the universe will hear, "I'm grateful I spend my money on junk food." Yipes! Instead you should say, "I feel healthy and fit. I always spend money on things and experiences that improve my life every day." See the difference?

- **State affirmations as if they have already happened.** "I am grateful that I have all the money I need to pay my bills on time each month" rather than, "I will have all the money I need next month..."
- **Attach a positive emotion to your affirmation**. I find gratitude to be a very powerful emotion to attach to affirmations for abundance but you can also feel excited, satisfied, powerful, or anything else that works for you.
- **Enjoy your affirmations.** Let them become more and more elaborate and exciting. Write them down.

And whenever you feel discouraged, pick up this little book and flip to an affirmation that makes you feel good. Then go out there and take action on your dreams.

Enjoy!

2
Affirmations to Create Prosperity

I am so grateful for the wellsprings of prosperity that flow to me from all directions.

I am blessed with boundless riches which I cheerfully share with all in need.

Jeanne Ellen Russell

I am amazed and excited at all the wonderful things I can do with my newfound wealth.

I enjoy my wealth which grows as I share it with my family, friends, and community.

I am so grateful for all the good things that my prosperity allows me to do and to have. I help those in need, travel, enjoy entertaining, and laugh when I think of the abundant life I lead.

Like a meandering stream, money flows to me gently, continually, and effortlessly.

Jeanne Ellen Russell

The universe conspires to make me rich and I use my wealth to help others and to create a life of worth.

I give thanks for the abundant life I lead, full of love from family, friends, and the community.

I am grateful for the abundance that permeates my life and positively affects all I touch and do.

Affirmations for Abundance

Like the flowers in spring, my bank account grows and the more I give, the more it overflows.

All my needs are met and I have plenty of money left over to share with family, friends, and community.

Affirmations for Abundance

I attract positive and profitable experiences each day.

Jeanne Ellen Russell

I have the capacity to work diligently and to persevere when working on projects that I care about.

Affirmations for Abundance

Projects that I care about are always profitable and satisfying to me.

Jeanne Ellen Russell

I have the confidence to pursue new opportunities of interest to me.

I love my work and my work loves me.

Jeanne Ellen Russell

People love to offer me new opportunities to make money and expand my effectiveness in the world.

I make the most of all positive opportunities which flow to me from all directions.

Jeanne Ellen Russell

I get satisfaction from pursuing my dreams.

Affirmations for Abundance

I dream big and my dreams expand as they come true.

Jeanne Ellen Russell

I am satisfied pursuing my dreams and get joy each day in striving to succeed in my efforts.

I feel powerful as I help others and helping others helps me.

Jeanne Ellen Russell

I enjoy the freedom to make my dreams come true.

Affirmations for Abundance

My prosperity is good for the world.

Jeanne Ellen Russell

I am grateful for the unexpected bounty which is mine by divine right.

Affirmations for Abundance

People love to reward me for doing my right work.

Jeanne Ellen Russell

Money flows to me from all directions.

I have so much money that it overflows and brings prosperity to everyone I meet.

Jeanne Ellen Russell

I feel secure and safe knowing that all my needs are met and I have overflowing abundance to share.

There is always more than enough.

Jeanne Ellen Russell

I magnetize money
then use it for good.

I am just where I am supposed to be and each seeming setback is a gift, the value of which will be revealed at the right time and place for me to appreciate and benefit.

Jeanne Ellen Russell

My overflowing wealth gives me the freedom to create the life of my dreams.

My cup runneth over as I receive money which I use to create freedom and happiness for myself and others in need.

Jeanne Ellen Russell

I am guided each day to hidden opportunities for abundance which I recognize and joyfully pursue.

Jeanne Ellen Russell

I have more than enough to meet my needs and what I don't need, I share.

Affirmations for Abundance

Jeanne Ellen Russell

Like a powerful waterfall, money rushes to me suddenly, inevitably, and miraculously transforming my life forever.

I receive and enjoy a serene and gentle steam of wealth which feeds and sustains me peacefully and effortlessly for many, many years to come.

3
Extra Tips to Create Abundance

Things you can do to attract prosperity

In addition to saying daily affirmations, you're probably already doing all the dumb guy normal stuff to make more money. Doing things like learning to manage the money you have, investing in your skills, starting an inspired business, or looking for a better job are all helpful activities (except maybe the "job" thing, but that's just me.) So in this chapter I'll share a few tips about things you can do to make your affirmations more powerful and effective.

Create a Manifestation Ritual

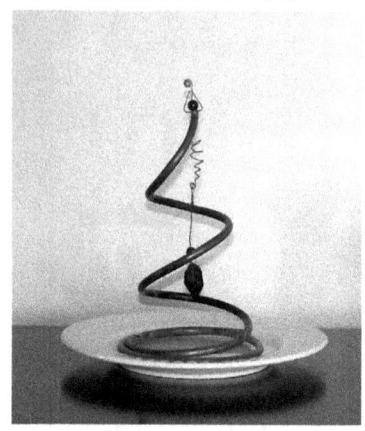

My Generator

Rituals are a collection of actions, performed in a specific order for their symbolic meaning. You can create a ritual in many ways. Regardless of form, it will have power if your intention is strong. And as you repeat the same ritual over and over, the power will grow.

I use what they call a generator in my manifestation ritual. It's made from a copper tube bent into a spiral. A copper wire with a crystal and amethyst attached hangs from the apex of the spiral. It is made of copper because copper is an excellent energy conductor. Many believe it has the power to actually amplify our thoughts. So using copper when attempting to manifest something new (like overflowing riches,) brings extra power to that manifestation.

    Materials I use:
        A generator
        A lighted candle
        Small pieces of paper
        Pens to write with
        A heat resistant dish or plate placed under the generator

I usually perform my manifestation ritual with friends. We start with a prayer. It might go something like: "We are gathered here to support each other in achieving our desires and humbly ask that we only manifest what is highest and best for all concerned." And then, as I'm a Christian, I might say, "in Jesus Christ's name," or something similar.

The generator is placed on the dish, in the center of the table. The candle is lit and placed next to the generator within reach of all participants. Each participant has paper and a pen. Affirmations may be written ahead of time or written out as part of the ritual.

We write our affirmations on the small pieces of paper. Three affirmations per participant works well. However, if all the participants are focused on manifesting money, then the number four is beneficial, either four total or four a piece. (In the feng shui tradition, four is the number for prosperity.)

After the prayer, participants take turns reading one affirmation aloud, lighting it with the candle, and placing the lit paper into the dish under the generator. Please be careful. We use thin sheets of paper which we roll up before lighting. As smoke spirals up out into the world each participant says, "…or something better" and/or, "let it be so."

We take turns, going around the table until all of the affirmations have been expressed. Then we give thanks and blow out the candle.

It may seem kind of 'woo woo' but this ritual feels really good when you do it and it is amazingly powerful.

Clear and Clean

The first time I heard about the electro-magnetic spectrum was in my high school chemistry class. At the time, I thought it sounded so cool – I still do. Unfortunately, science has never been my strong suit. As far as I'm concerned, when I flip the switch and the light comes on, it's magic. So to me, trying to explain electro-magnetic energy is probably not wise. So I'll just say this. Every person, animal, and thing emits energy and that energy affects the people, places, and things around it.

We all carry and release energy. When we say affirmations, we are sending a certain type of energy out into the universe and it is interacting and attracting other positive energy to us.

The chair I'm sitting on also affects the energy in the room where I write. Everything affects everything.

Energy and prosperity

Dirty cluttered spaces create dirty cluttered energy. I mean, how can you honestly expect to attract prosperity and abundance if you live in a sty? You've got to make a space for the abundance you want to attract.

In Feng Shui, the ancient Chinese system of arranging our space to positively attract helpful energy, our homes are divided into nine sections called the Ba Gua.

Basically if you want to attract prosperity into your life, you're going to make sure your prosperity section, which is the back left section of your home, is clean and uncluttered.

If you are having trouble covering your monthly expenses, you'll also want to clean and de-clutter the middle left section of your house which is the family section, and also affects your ability to pay your monthly bills.

There are many beneficial colors and objects that you can add to these spaces to increase prosperity but that's another book. Learn more about Feng Shui on my website: www.fengshuitoolkit.com.

After you clean, clear, and create a special environment in you prosperity corner, you can sit in it to recite your affirmations for abundance. Try it.

Visualize

This tip can be used in conjunction with the next tip about writing down your desires. You need to be able to see yourself achieving what you want before you can actually get it. This may seem obvious and basic, but it is amazing how many people don't even allow themselves to dream about what they want, let alone do anything to get it. I can use myself as an example.

I was the youngest of four children raised by a divorced mom. We were poor. We weren't raised poor. We weren't on public assistance or anything like that but my mom worked two jobs and struggled to support us as best she could. We couldn't afford yearly vacations like my friends' families but we all went to college. We paid for it with student loans, scholarships, and work/study.

Consequently, I had a poverty mentality until I was about 30 years old without even realizing it. One manifestation of this was the fact that it never occurred to me that I could own a home. Rich people bought houses. How would I ever come up with a 20% down-payment on a house? Like many kids from "broken homes," I had a real problem with delayed gratification. I knew I could never save up the thousands of dollars necessary for a down payment, let alone convince anyone to give me a mortgage.

I had a decent government job. People I worked with owned homes but it never occurred to me that I was as wealthy as they were. I was sure I would never own a home. I didn't even dream of buying a house. And of course, if I never even allowed myself to dream about that kind of prosperity, there was no way I was ever going to achieve it.

Luckily everything changed on March 23, 1993 when my son, Daniel, was born. Suddenly I had a reason to dream big which enabled me to visualize a life that was richer. While on some level I never thought I deserved great riches, I knew that he deserved everything the world had to offer. I bought my first house when he was two.

I have come a long way from the poor girl who would never be rich enough to own her own home. But I still have to work on my internal dialog. That's why I say affirmations. I need them and they do help. It's not magic but it feels like magic to me.

Spend time allowing yourself to visualize your perfect life. Think about everything you want, not just money. After all, most of us want money to achieve something else. It's not really money that we long for but what we think money will bring. We want an abundance of freedom, security, and love. We think money can do that for us. And to a certain extent it can. But of course money in itself is not the real goal. So visualize what you really want. Think of the lives you can touch and the good you can do and the interests you will have time to pursue with your newfound weath. And enjoy the process of visualizing all that you want. Then use the next tip.

Write Your Wishes - Every Day

Research has shown that when we write things down, even if we never look at them again, we have an easier time of remembering them. They get planted somewhere in our subconscious mind. And remembering our dreams or goals, even subconsciously, helps us recognize opportunities and stay focused on what is important to us. There is something almost magical about the power of the written word. That's why I recommend writing your favorite affirmations in your own handwriting. It doesn't have to be pretty or even legible, although re-reading positive thoughts back in times of stress can be very helpful.

Another wonderful bit of advice is to start a dream journal, in which you write about your ideal life as if you were already living it. Be specific. Be outrageous. Think about what your life would look like if the world were perfect - and then top it in your journal.

Writing down your wishes can be very rewarding – both spiritually and financially. The universe works in mysterious ways and written wishes are powerful. This truth was brought home to me in a delightful way when I came across an old notebook I had used while reading *Wishcraft* by Barbara Sher. *Wishcraft* contains all sorts of exercises and advice geared towards helping the reader figure out what they want in life and how to go about getting it. Anyway, one of the early exercises has you describe a typical day in the life of your dreams. When I did the exercise, I was a government contractor living in the city and working a typical work week doing typical government work. In the exercise I described a very different life where each day was unique and I was working on projects I loved in a beautiful old house close to nature. In my dream world, I had many creative outlets and I was, among other things, an actor. When I came across my notebook, over 10 years later, I was living in my current home which is an old house in the heart of the Shenandoah Valley where I run my creative services and publishing businesses. I am close to nature. In fact, I have a labyrinth in my back yard where I sit and meditate surrounded my chirping birds and hopping bunnies. Each day is unique and I am very involved in the local community theater, where I enjoy acting. The only significant difference between what I wrote in my dream exercise and what I have in my life now is the fact that in my dream, I was married, and in life, I am not – yet.

If the idea of writing out your dreams appeals to you and you want more a specific instructions on how to do it. I recommend you read *Write it Down, Make it Happen*, by Henriette Anne Klauser, Ph.D.

Affirmations for Abundance

My final advice for creating abundance in your own life is to dream big, give thanks, and enjoy the ride. As Mame, one of my all time favorite characters in fiction once said, "Life is a Banquet and most poor suckers are starving to death!" Don't let that be you. Create your own menu and then enjoy the feast!

About The Author

Jeanne Russell is an entrepreneur, publisher, mom, actor, activist, teacher, hostess, and friend. She first became interested in the power of affirmations when she read Napoleon Hill's classic, *Think and Grow Rich* and met Barbara Winter, author of *Making a Living without a Job*. After attending Winter's seminar also called Making a Living without a Job (several times), Jeanne resigned from her position as a government contractor and moved to the Shenandoah Valley in Virginia to pursue making her living on her own terms. To this end, Jeanne runs a creative services business, publishes several websites, and holds seminar classes on topics of interest to her. She co-hosted the *Just Say It!* radio show on WSVG in Mt Jackson, VA from 2006 to 2009 and produced the *Valley of the Stars* radio show on *95.3 FM The River* before that. Her new book on natural cleaning and feng shui, *Toss the Toxins,* is scheduled for publication in October 2011. Jeanne continues to pursue all her dreams one after another. Life is sweet and affirmations are powerful.

www.ingramcontent.com/pod-product-compliance
Lightning Source LLC
Chambersburg PA
CBHW071416040426
42444CB00009B/2271